THE PORTAGE POETRY SERIES

Series Titles

Always a Body
Molly Fuller

Bowed As If Laden With Snow
Megan Wildhood

Silent Letter
Gail Hanlon

New Wilderness
Jenifer DeBellis

Fulgurite
Catherine Kyle

The Body Is Burden and Delight
Sharon White

Bone Country
Linda Nemec Foster

Not Just the Fire
R.B. Simon

Monarch
Heather Bourbeau

The Walk to Cefalù
Lynne Viti

The Found Object Imagines a Life: New and Selected Poems
Mary Catherine Harper

Naming the Ghost
Emily Hockaday

Mourning
Dokubo Melford Goodhead

Messengers of the Gods: New and Selected Poems
Kathryn Gahl

After the 8-Ball
Colleen Alles

Careful Cartography
Devon Bohm

Broken On the Wheel
Barbara Costas-Biggs

Sparks and Disperses
Cathleen Cohen

Holding My Selves Together: New and Selected Poems
Margaret Rozga

Lost and Found Departments
Heather Dubrow

Marginal Notes
Alfonso Brezmes

The Almost-Children
Cassondra Windwalker

Meditations of a Beast
Kristine Ong Muslim

Praise for
Always a Body

"*Always a Body* is sharply tuned to a moment that is as intoxicating as it is menacing. Lift the corner of Molly Fuller's unrelentingly bold and confident language and find an Escher painting, an algorithm, a vellum, a forceful indictment of the mishandling of bodies staged in a world that exploits and disregards them, where both cells and thighs calve like glaciers, where the body 'is pain / is wildness, is vicious witness to disappearance.' These poems are desperately sexy and beautifully deranged — dare to live with them a while and they will disturb you, comfort you, and change you."

—Michelle Lewis
author of *Animul/Flame*

"With a 'ferocious shudder,' Molly Fuller's *Always a Body* bursts like a firework with poems that destroy and foresee, articulating the desire of Hélène Cixous with a new insurgent writing that wilts and blooms in turns like a game of red rover: play and violence, call and response, words and bodies. Medical indices, whale falls, anxiety, family genealogy, chronic pain, and internet culture make up the world of *Always a Body* with 'the tears, the rain, the mud, the ghosts.' Fuller's writing is fluent in the language of critique but never bogged down by it; every crisp syllable erupts with courage, love, confidence, and endurance."

—Andrew Rihn
author of *Revelation: An Apocalypse in Fifty-Eight Fights*

"Molly Fuller's new collection is as tender as it is precise. These musical poems—that move with a rhythm much like a pulse through a body—explore desire, pain, grief, and pleasure. And they do so in a space where form meets function meets something beyond. This book reminds us 'to love and love / what is rust and dust' until we are able to trust the tenderness that Fuller so often reminds us 'will be enough to get us through.'"

—Nicole Robinson
author of *Without a Field Guide*

"Sometimes it seems that Molly Fuller is channeling Gertrude Stein: 'The salt the salt the salt / skin a beginning of when / of when of when of when / a mother becomes a mother / a woman becomes / a lover and a man is neither.' Her experiments with form—innovative use of line spacing, columns—invite us to read both horizontally and vertically, the same way we read a fragile human body struggling to be whole. Though there's a lot of pain and sorrow in these poems, there's also a movement toward a life with its many rewards. When we read 'The smell of peonies drifts in the open window as I unwind my hair, letting it unfurl toward you like new roots,' we realize that what we've read as an extended elegy might also be a quiet resurrection."

—Rick Campbell
author of *Sometimes the Light*

"This amniotic book of elements—salt, water, body, rust, loss—stutter-thumps its elegy and praise with tender details, the way the body carries its facts, the drowning, the pain, the chemical load, the spines of our books, the spines of our lovers. 'My body is mine / to mine and mind. My pain is my own body. My lover is a body, is not pain, is not / my body, is my body wanting,' Molly Fuller writes, painting the body, painting the body as common denominator, as art and memory, as every reason."

—Karen Schubert
author of *The Compost Reader*

"In *Always a Body*, we encounter and reencounter the dialogism of the body holding together and coming apart. What holds the body together is not necessarily durable material. The thread holding these poems together is sturdy and deep-rooted in capturing the atmospheric ephemeral, in making us feel in familiar ways where the body and where our selves fuse and where we break."

—Angie Mazakis
author of *I Was Waiting to See What You Would Do First*

ALWAYS A BODY

poems

MOLLY FULLER

Cornerstone Press
Stevens Point, Wisconsin

Cornerstone Press, Stevens Point, Wisconsin 54481
Copyright © 2023 Molly Fuller
www.uwsp.edu/cornerstone

Printed in the United States of America by
Point Print and Design Studio, Stevens Point, Wisconsin

Library of Congress Control Number: 2022952050
ISBN: 979-8-9869663-8-0

Cornerstone Press titles are produced in courses and internships offered by the
Department of English at the University of Wisconsin–Stevens Point.

DIRECTOR & PUBLISHER   EXECUTIVE EDITOR
Dr. Ross K. Tangedal   Jeff Snowbarger

SENIOR EDITORS
Lexie Neeley, Monica Swinick, Kala Buttke

PRESS STAFF
Ellie Atkinson, Carolyn Czerwinski, Hannah Fenrick, Patrick Fogarty, Angela Green,
Cal Henkens, Brett Hill, Julia Kaufman, Amanda Leibham, Maria Scherer, Abbi
Wasielewski

for Robert, my first reader

Also by Molly Fuller:

For Girls Forged by Lightning: Prose & Other Poems
Tender the Body
The Neighborhood Psycho Dreams of Love

Poems

One

Two

Three

One

A Girl Is Always a Body

Mostly a body is a body is a holding together.
What is a girl is a girl is a girl that is mostly pain?

What is a body that is mostly pain?
What is pain? What is pain if there is no body?

What is a body that is no longer a body?
What is a ghost? What is a girl a girl

wandering in the forest? What is a tree
if it is burning? What is a forest if it is ash?

What is rain if there is no water? A body
is a container for water. What is a girl

a girl if she is no longer a girl but always
a body? What is a body that is pain? What is pain?

What does it hurt if there is nobody? What is a ghost?
What is useless? What are signs of loss? An empty

container a burning tree ashes ashes a ghost in the forest.
Mostly a body is a body is a ritual holding together.

What is ice if it is water? What is water if it is salt?
What is a body if it is pain?

A body is a ghost is a girl is a forest on fire.
What is fire is inferno devouring ferocious incandescence

luminosity charring combustion. What is fire without air?
Bonfire bones ash coal ember tinder dust dust dust.

Most of the bodies are ghosts, women are forest fires.
Bodies are bodies are dust holding together. Most

bodies are containers. What's a girl if she's not a girl
but always a body? Is it water if it is salt? Is it a forest

fire? A girl is a container is a ghost is a body is a
forest on fire is a tree that is igniting. A burning forest

is a girl is a ghost is a body is a body holding together
is a girl a girl a girl.

Good Girl

socks are matched and mostly clean

sockets of eyes are filled with green

marbles that roll away from prying

fingers and the tears roll soundless

in the Ohio city where she is crying

how sorrow is/is not what you know

a black crow picking the carcass clean

a good Midwestern girl who is made

of milk and corn and the cracked rim

of used bicycle tires and corroded bolts

the thread of soft graying clouds always

promising rain and the delivery of rust

in the eye of the needle is a closed fist

How to Abandon a City

The loneliness is not lonely, but it is easier to deceive yourself.
Dark curvy roads and spindly wheels and lovers are dangerous.

So many things have a history of seeming like something that
I want to call *goodness*. Historic houses, wombs, the Model T Ford.

Apple devices updating overnight. String theory being carefully
explained in the next room. I'm coming to understand spoiled milk

is mostly *in process* of spoiling before the thing is actually spoiled.
Spill it and we cry; spoil it and we pour it out. My womb is cramping,

blood clots are traveling up and down and down and up my legs.
The realty company wants to sell us a story like that one about a girl

who got the pill stuck in her throat and it melted through her esophagus.
Was that really real? The ghost in the house that haunts me is as real

as I am. Are you dead? Are you dead? Are you dead? I ask Google
and the ghosts in the halls of all the haunted houses in this city answer

with low moans. The houses with the ghosts. The ghosts in the hallways.
The spirits stay here stay here stay here and the dry cough cough cough

in the next town over has already packed up and left this history behind
is not my ghost not my ghost not my ghost not my lonely ghost story.

Sara Says Ghosts are Real

I feel her body leave my body
and we're the ghosts here now

All the trees and ground are scorched

Our cancer cells are most likely increasing
Our skin is tender on the forest floor

Our bodies are tinder among sticks

We are slowly trying to forget
metastasizing cells

Our white skin shines in the dark

I feel her body leave her own body
and we are ghosts

Every tree is burning

Leaves are fire orange, the sky is smoke
Pine needles whisper past our faces

The tears, the rain, the mud, the ghosts

Endurance

Sara says there is always the wanting like an ache   It never leaves us
after the ones we love do   After they leave us behind, alone on this earth

There is so much falling into and out of and hoping to be caught
and the rocks are breaking beneath our feet, can you feel them?

Can you feel the rocks shifting?   This planet is not our home
We don't live here anymore   Sara says we are visitors, we are

plunderers, we have taken too much and the plasticity of our love
is not our only sin in this world   Sara talks and talks and I love the way

her mouth moves on the softness of my body   I love the way her mouth
feels on my mouth   I take Sara's hand   I hold her in my arms   I tell her

this tender moment can last, it can last I tell her knowing that it is fleeting
even as I'm saying it   I can feel her body leaving my body and already

we are becoming ghosts to each other and all the trees are on fire
and the carcinogens in our breasts are multiplying as we stroke each other

softly, embers glowing in the darkness of the night   Sara says she understands
my soft feelings   She says she wants to protect them and hold on to me

as if we were falling   I say that's nice hon but I'm too far down already
I can't see the forest or the trees I say   Sara looks through me   Right through

me and says the wanting will never end, it won't ever end   she says but
it will become bearable   I close my eyes and see her   I always see her

She pulls me toward her and my skin is cracking and fevered   I say
this is nice, but I know I've already messed up   I can only see the trees

are burning   Sara looks at me   I can find her with my eyes closed   Sara
says she always wants to feel pain, or else why still live?   She says that

to be alive is to suffer   She asks me, don't you feel the water rising?
We are robbers, she says, we put in so much effort, think the flexibility

of our killing will save us   It is not our only sin in this world   Sara
talks and talks and I want her mouth to move on the softness of my body

I love the way she makes my body feel   My skin breaks and heats up
Weightless as the sea, my cells constellations of fire   This love is unbearable

X-Ray

Sara says Justin doesn't care about lead in the water.
He says they can give you cancer

so don't even worry about your Fitbit
always knowing exactly where you are.

I ask who is *they*. Sara shrugs. Maybe
it's Google or Amazon or this heavy air quality.

Sara says that Justin says when we *Love* most like capital L
it doesn't matter so much that the world is unhealthy.

I don't say anything. He calls us lipstick lesbians.
He asks who wears the pants.

Labels embody bullying, but I know
his meanness will attract her.

Sara says with a calm sobriety, don't worry
about the lead in the water. The world

is unhealthy, malignant she says and if we just
love everyone enough the Earth will heal she says.

I don't know if she knows how much bullshit this is
but since I'm trying so hard I keep quiet

about all the toxicity and microplastics and the rising sea
level, about my stretch marks, my own insecurities.

When I look at Sara I see a body that *knows* things
and I'm much less worried about what she calls the pooch

of her stomach after two kids, the loss of muscles there.
I see a soft pillow I rest my cheek against trying

to stave off my own fragmentations.
Justin is looking at Sara, radiation in his gaze.

He bisects her like an x-ray.
My bones grow heavy with lead.

Hands Falling Like Two Birds

And Angel, Sara says, is *fine*. Sara says she remembers Angel's pale dancer legs, paler than the beige-white tights she wore. Sara says *It was a brief affair*. Sara says she *loved everything*, but *everything wasn't enough* for Angel and that was *who Angel was*. I like the way Sara describes Angel, the spillage of Angel's thinking. I picture Angel dancing, her legs gleaming, the Milky Way splashing, spilling milk, the inside of a gardenia. White legs falling, falling like twin birch branches. *Angel says,* Sara says, *it was good. Says her legs were flashing creamy white thighs.* Says Angel *says it's just nuts in a nutshell.* Says *she's all like, it's all like this and like that and she's like this.* I love how Sara describes how Angel thinks out loud. *And it's not what you have that matters so much as how you move* Angel said to Sara. *How you move, how you dance it out, don't keep it inside but let it become you. Your body is you* Angel said to Sara. I can see Angel's hands flutter like two birds, no, not like birds, not like birds at all, but like something I've seen before and I'm trying, really trying to remember in the back of my mind. Not something I can remember really, but something that I just know, like down in my bones, but not just in my bones. In my cells. In the mitochondria of my cells. The nuclei of them as they split and cleave and halve like the glaciers are doing right now. *Calving* the scientists say. And I think about art and beauty and Angel. Sara says *her legs were so white* she says *her legs were so soft. Like bread, like the soft inside of a loaf of bread* and she describes wanting to lay her head down on Angel's thighs and weep. I know that feeling. The feeling, the wanting, the desire to weep over thighs that are like warm soft bread. And over ice melting. And over a sea rising like hot tears in my throat.

Almost Perfect Stillness

Truth is true with you. I said that I cannot justify myself
from absolute zero. You say it's too cold down here

to take your hand away, but I think it's too hot. I think
that's only the beginning. You say that you cannot choose

me because you cannot choose. Sometimes you are
the worst person in history and sometimes you are

another. It is said that everyone has been robbed at least
once. After such an experience, you will feel charged.

The focus of your life is no longer on your personal nature;
it is an addition within you that is more than just your own

life. Not everyone does math, mainly because not everyone
has the same number. I don't really protect myself enough.

It is hard to hold your own hand partly because the atoms
that make up matter never stop moving. I am sure anyone

who has been abducted by aliens can be at least once.
Funny, but we all know how to steal someone's identity.

The Graces Prefer Those Who Wear Flowers

Her mouth is an open
   Oh, her hair an aureole

she is so beautiful
   what wanting

dying and drowning in
   the opening petals of flowers

unfolding of tea leaves
   ice sheets converging

animals vanishing
   her mouth is open

her hair a red poppy field
   desire, desire

what is blooming and
   what is dead

what is this disappearance
   she is breathing

endurance is unfolding
   splendor of ignition

her skin burns my skin
   like too much salt

I have left her so many
   times to survive

the wanting
   leaving is like

the dying sea
     the salt

rising
     the salt fills my mouth

there is nothing but salt and more salt
     and no water

what is this unfolding
     her mouth is uncompromising

her legs are open
     the mouth of an orchid

her body cleaving my body
     I am dry clay

I am desert
     thirsty, thirsty

It's Fine. I'm Fine. Everything is Fine.

In a single night in Texas someone destroyed half a million bees. All that sweetness gone. Though I am far away, there is an outburst of rage. I feel the blood pulse in my throat, and I'm afraid. My heart is full of fear.

You say *What do you mean?* I focus on each color, and you are everything, so there is no color. *Dear friend, dear one, dearest* I think. Slippage is so easy. I don't know if you ever mean what you say. *How is your body?* you ask. I'm thinking I have been infinitely located. Embodied outside of my body.

We are lying on a wooden deck scattered with fall leaves. All the colors of autumn and you and I intertwined. I feel every inch of you and I shake. *Five hundred thousand levels of honey erased in an instant* I say. You say *What do you mean?* I want to say *It's frightful to think that love can die as quickly as a single bee.* I want to say *All that sweetness gone.*

Shelf Life

I say to my friend *Your hair reminds me of the night sky.* I want to say *You are beautiful. Lay off the face paint.* But I know she won't. She makes fat jokes with her body as the punch line. I have already fucked my eating plan for today by nibbling the edges of this cookie that I snatched off your plate while you weren't looking. Now, I will eat this whole cake that I bought at the cake store on 4th. I would offer you some, but it is one task I have set myself that I plan on completing. My own body often lets me down. It feels the way I imagine soaking in hydrochloric acid would feel, but I don't actually have an inkling. Did you know that all of our cells regenerate every seven years? I am comforted by this thought: *This particular weariness has an expiration date.*

We Measure by the Second Hand Circling

tick of breaths in / breaths out
                      water rising / receding

the way young children
gather daisies
to fashion into necklaces, into crowns

pick petals off
                      one by one by one
sing riddles, make up love's depths predicted
by flower
                      stamen, pistil, thin leaves arcing around
                      the tender yellow button
                      praise of tulips, of a lily's soft unfurling

the butterfly / bee / hummingbird

                      the nectar

the sweet buzz and hum   a wing / a whir

              a pearl in a nest of moss

the precarious hope of an egg

                              *

late May / early June

from greening leaves curling open
moth larvae on the end of thin silk threads
hung like hair ribbons
filaments shimmering in dusty light

                              *

we want to feel the wondrous

the way water leaves us
evaporates into clouds, into air

the way a bird's small body
curves into feathered flight

Mission to Mars

Bodies are like fire

both ash and smoke

at once as solid as wood

spirit as ephemeral as mist

skin and bones and a heaviness

that we call upon to stay

feet planted in time

gravity holding us transfixed

on an ever-moving planet

Bodies are bodies are bodies

even when shot into space

Imagine this sudden freedom

from stricture of convention

our bones growing lighter

our corporeality no longer

the reality

We would watch water float

see droplets hover in thin air

look upon an Earth so imperceptible

as unfathomable as what we call soul

And is this floating sphere of water

really *water* any longer?

Is this air that holds

that we cannot breathe

even *air*?

Would that which is dying

stars, a planet, a dear friend

feel much different from the

red-rocked surface of Mars?

We use an old language to try

and describe the indescribable

to explain ashes to ashes

the rings of Saturn

a body's return to dust

Violent Wonder

I forget my body is a body until I open my mouth to let out the cold.
Like a stalk of grass calibrating the weight of a hollow-boned bird

all of my pain is a ferocious shudder falling down my spine, a xylophone of wasps,
an aviary of cracks and fissures, a simple holding together of skin over bones.

The thin stalk breaks. The once-balanced bird on the tall grass stalk becomes a bee
floating in blue sky. A single pink helium balloon deflating in an empty room.

My body is pain, my pain embodied. My body violent fracture, jarring of buzzing,
a wax castle melting, honey of a stolen jar, ajar, a barely holding together.

I am alive but cannot create a life. The savage wonder of my ovaries
leave me barely able to mouth my pain. A woman with black hair and blue eyes

once held me as I doubled over. Love is and is not about blood.
Some men will say they don't want a woman to bleed on them.

Blood is sometimes a violence. These kinds of men are often brutal
and will say it is love. This kind of love is always bloody.

This kind of man hurt this woman and took her child. Violence is often a man,
is my twisted ovaries, is not the empty table where this woman whose body

was as small as a doll once held me up. Her hair was blue-black and her eyes
were blue streams and there was a lost baby in the beehive of her mouth.

My attraction to her was both savage and tender, surprised as I was by my own
body's impulsive wildness. The way I could disappear into her. This disappearance

was a wildness to her and a wonder to me. Wonder is rapturous is a bird in flight
is the violence of revelation is the pain of returning to the body. My body is pain,

is wildness, is vicious witness to disappearance, is brutal and beautiful flower,
is the blooming blood of my un-child is the bird in the hive of my mouth.

The Cherry Tree Blessing

1: I'm not writing this to make you happy

The grass does not grow there, green and fragrant, springy
underneath your bare feet just for you—a cherry tree does
not blossom, raining petals down upon your dark hair just
because you want it to.

I nestle my head in your shoulder, on a blanket spread
beneath a tree, knowing that sometimes love is like dying.
It's the inability to breathe, to know oneself outside
of another. I know what it is like to be consumed.

I'm not writing this for you.

2: Benediction

The hollow bones in my wrists, squeeze them tightly
between your two hands, as if you were preparing
to bind them with rope, until you can feel the marrow
inside the bone, until you can feel the gentle pressure
of the blood pumping beneath the skin.

Stay, you would say.

My skin, translucent as tissue paper in places. If you
could read the veins underneath, like a story written
just for you alone, I wonder what translations of blood,
and tissue, and bone we might create. What metaphors
we could conceive, what the narrative of our two bodies
would become.

I imagine the lines you'd write over me, dripping ink
on my back, my thighs, my calves, marking every part
of me, trailing your words beyond the edges of my skin
like droplets of blood onto the white sheets.

My body, nothing but a canvas of skin stretched over
bone to return to ash too soon.

Sprinkle my ashes under a tree; make it a cherry tree
blooming in the spring, the pink petals floating through
the air, raining down over the dark heads of two lovers
kissing on a blanket.

Let them stay happy.

3: Immolation

We meet in the doorway.

There are no words as you lead me to the bed.
You undress me, lay me down on soft white sheets,
rub oil slowly over my bare skin. The scent
of orchids fills the room. The ache for you,
a blessing, splits me apart with desire.

Years and years splinter and fracture between us, but
a body remembers in stillness, in disintegration,
the dissolving into you. I cradle your face between
my hands, a prayer: we will be good to each other here.

Blossoms from a cherry tree fall to the ground, over
and over again.

Two

The River Will Bear You

Picture: raindrops
merging on a window pane

: stream disappears into lake
The river you love so well

can hold your chest down
Image: dogs struggling

to crack or gnaw a bone
: riding an ancient bicycle

before rubber wheels
Your beloved river swells

against your breast
Picture: dogs trying

to cheat at cards
: A quick rotation,

rotator cuff disjoints,
cartilage cracks and spurs

Dams break, the house wins
You assume when you enter

the river your flesh will
enter the river, when

you get in the water you
immerse yourself whole

skin bones teeth soul
Photograph: wolves fighting

breaking bones for marrow
: lower now, into the muck

Water gathers against water
contains break and last breath

the heft and the weight
of the body in silence

Picture the sunlit surface
: minnows flicker, ripple

Calibrations

A blue whale's heart rate is calculated at 37 beats
per minute. Measurement is described as intense,

involving extensive coordination. Descent
into the ocean and the pressure a human body

is subjected to is an additional atmosphere, twice
as much as human lungs are used to. A man holds

his breath for eleven minutes. Depths complicate,
compress and shrink the air-containing spaces

in body and brain. Oxygen starvation feels like
euphoria, like experiencing something miraculous.

It takes two seconds to pump the 220 liters of blood
a blue whale circulates with every heartbeat. There

cannot possibly be a larger animal, the heart cannot
grow fast enough for a greater creature to survive.

A woman holds her breath for nine minutes.
The sensation of rising. Water, water, sunlight,

air. A pulse in the ears. The astonishing
violence as breath fills her lungs, her heart.

Metamorphosis

Fish without memory / fish with memory

water flows over / oxygen is extracted

                              branchial arch, visceral arch, gill arch

                                    cartilaginous (vertebrate animal)

transitory we understand

we are becoming / we are something other

                                          mandible, hyoid bone, larynx

                                                lamellae / capillarity

gives way to periodic breathing

out of the womb

                                              like a fish on dry land

                              anadramous / what do they remember?

Flocculation (creaming / sedimentation)

permeability / amniotic

                                    subsidence (tendency of a liquid)

                                                (surface tension)

too often we forget

there is no scale for our memories

Fractals of Skin Hunger

we are mostly water

everything we love

precious and scarce

vast, flowing, unknowable

ever more longing

awestruck

ferocity

unthinkable to lose

such a world: wetlands, corals

forests, mangroves, fish, seagrass

no restraint of the habit

to be exploited recklessly

thorough enmeshing

water collects other water

a fragile tendency

holds bodies together

skin against skin

gathers us toward recursion

reunion of circling

lichen on granite

patterning desire

after our violent natures

friction, altercation,

alteration, fission, recalibration,

irreversibly, you said

always, always, always

Prayer

when is water no longer   water but salt left behind?
water is always water   unless it is not water at all

the moon is not   water   but gravity   that holds
and pulls   and curves into bodies   a child is a bit

of moon a bit of water a border a bridge   a body
what is a border?   what is a cage?   is a body a border?

is a child a weapon?   a body is a cage is a child
is a border is a body is a weapon   is a moon

is gravity and salt is what water left behind   a child
is what is disappeared   water is a body   still

containing gravity   and a child   is a moon
in the mother's belly   a rock   in the father's hand

a body   is a knife   is the blood   left behind
is the salt the salt the salt   we sprinkle

on our bloody meat   the mother   a prayer   we say
before we eat   the father   the lookout   the moon

is the table   is the water   we pray will wash us clean

This Resembles a Funeral Ritual

scarcity of trees
room for all
toxicity of paint
exposure
farther from windows
doors (which can fly open)
(which can cave in)
extraction works
trickling water
soda is purified
unthinkable levels
flesh from bone
extract DNA
(keepsake locket)
burned seaweed
barilla (or salicornia)
blisters
the body
fed to the sky

open floor plan
(especially at holidays)
dependent on individual
deeper and lower
(which can shatter)
exterior walls
better your odds
through ashes
hardwood fire
leaves white crystals
(an intimacy of cutting)
survivable exchanges
from marrow
act of generosity
coastal plants
dried kelp
flat feet
(in manageable pieces)
to the birds

What's the Harm of Coming into Existence?

I am afraid of immutable hands like a split between sleeping me

and awake me But must edges always be edges?

The shell in the palm of your hand symbolizes the ocean

Minerals remain colonized by suspension

fat-depleted bones of whale falls

have been mapped and labeled

what is unfolding is unmapped

and sheltering sedimentation of a decomposing

inherent part of sentient existence Do we bear witness?

The bones will change from

recognizable to unrecognizable will mark the season

everything unseen everything silent

New World (Arrival)

Thought currents (electric conduction) bloom (rose buds) carefully tended in rows (plastic flower gardens) would render (yield) continuous human (specious) presence unnecessary (dispensable) Functional equivalent (fractions) mutate the reversal (suburbs) dismantling the system (weed whackers) of deceits (picket fences) Disinformation (retinal scans) paradigms (surveillance state) flipping off security cameras (they saw that) can you really steal money from an ATM? (money isn't real) An ATM doesn't differentiate your hand from a pick-pocket's hand (yet) Access to keys (musical scores) for locked doors (when one closes) not codes for missiles (droning) salt shaker (grains of rice) on the nightstand signals (ghosts) a warding off (we bring our superstitions) Do not enter (another door supposedly opens) the threshold (carry me over) without spilling salt (gifted rosary on the mirror) over your left (remaining) shoulder Enlighten the lunar (Mr. Moon: a child's song) economic dashboard (offshore accounts) hopes of mimicking (look at those dumb graphs) capable (capitalism is a pyramid scheme) human existence (tenderly imagined) Explorations of space (time is a continuum) using wonder and curiosity (my dear utopian friend)

Murmuration

We thread the needle to
we thread the needle through

We lick our lips
we thread the thread to do the job

Thread will do to suture wounds
that are manageable

Now we link arms
Which way does the wind

come in? Through the cracks
Perhaps we should ask about

balance We are told to want
less Our winged precarity

Rust and blood are both red
We call across the wind

Red Rover we call
Rust over we call

We thread the needle to
we thread the needle through

We wash our hands
we move our lips

Together to put together
clasped surface area tension

Stripe house split house
as the crow flies

It is all precarious
it is a nuisance

to love and love
what is rust and dust

and turns to coal
to ash as we murmur

and clap hands
and demand another turn

You Are in It and I Am in It

There are probably six
people exactly like us in the
whole universe. I must admit:
I haven't heard anything from
mine. This is probably the self-
fulfilling stage in the genetic
code. Single species. Places
of evolutionary novelty. Sonar
mapping has not gotten us as
far as we would like. Swirling the
glass of ice sipping on pink
cocktail umbrella
drinks calling each other baby.
Slumping forward
in the sand until we are
sheltering underneath
the dying palm trees
and coconuts dropping
on our heads like bowling
balls. Jogging memories of
better times. We lick the sugar
rim and stay in our oblivions.

Collapse

1.

Honey bees, bats, swallows, crayfish, trout, pigeons, alligators are all sensitive to toxins. Animal sentinels must have responses measurable to the hazard. Rabbits check for leaks at plants for Sarin nerve production. Handlers wear protective gear (See Fig. 1). Canaries dead in cages signal unsafe air conditions to miners (See Fig. 2). See also: Colony Collapse Disorder.

2.

Chronic fatigue syndrome (CFS), Myalgic Encephalomyelitis (ME). *Algic* adjectival form of *algia*, meaning pain. My shortened form of *myo*, meaning muscle. Not just being tired as from lack of sleep. Possible triggers: smoke, auto exhaust, perfume, insecticides, new carpet, chlorine. No effective proven treatments. Abnormal blood levels of hormones produced in hypothalamus, pituitary and adrenal glands detected. Also called Systemic Exertion Intolerance Disease (SEID). Long-term, chronic, affects multiple body systems.

3.

Known Endocrine disruptors: Diethylstilbestrol (the synthetic estrogen DES), dioxin and dioxin-like compounds, polychlorinated, biphenyls (PCBs), DDT and other pesticides, plastic bottles, metal food cans, detergents, toys, flame retardants, cosmetics, food. See also: Infant formula. Effects include: lowered fertility, increased incidence of endometriosis, and some cancers. Greatest risk during prenatal and early postnatal development. Formation most susceptible: organ systems, neural systems.

4.

In this study, possible relationships between and in combination with—. Chloramine, chlorine and fluoride; disinfectants added to drinking water reduce micro-organisms like bacteria and viruses.

Lead, Chromium 6, detected. Lead is seeped through aging infrastructure, ancient pipes 80-100+ years old. Corrosion control treatment needed. Lead consumption can affect heart, kidneys and nerves.

5.

Risk from radiation for most people may develop. Parental exposure leads to six multifactorial diseases: anencephaly, cleft palate, cleft lip with or without cleft palate, club foot, polydactyly (additional finger or toe), and syndactyly (fusion of two or more fingers or toes).These abnormalities accounted for 445 of the 594 (75%) malformed infants (see Table 3). Also, increased incidences of imbalance in the autonomic nervous system.

6.

Thick dust clouds from falling debris blinded the miners trapped for six hours. The group attempted escape via ventilation shafts but were unsuccessful due to missing ladders which were meant to be in place according to safety codes. The first group out looked ready to collapse at any moment. The second group included those with medical problems, older people, and those with psychological issues. The third group were deemed the most mentally tough with "nerves like steel. "The company responsible for the accident struck a deal with survivors, citing the cause of the collapse as "systemic failure." (See Fig. 2).

Q & A

Q: Can you survive cryogenic freezing?
How much does it cost to cryogenically freeze yourself?
Has anyone been cryogenically frozen and thawed?

A: No adult human has ever been revived
from temperatures far below freezing.
Cryonics patients are cared for
in the expectation that future technology,
especially molecular nanotechnology,
will be available to reverse damage
associated with the cryonics process.

A: A person who can be resuscitated is not dead.

Dust

Planets and stars.
Between the black oak

branches, patterns
made from light.

Friends, friends
the world is

a deeply moving place
but we are not in

quiet space.
The world prays

to a burning star.
The sea is of salt.

The desert is of dust.
We stay inside deep

cells and safe pockets,
forgetting how isolate,

particulate, vulnerable,
how like grains of sand

we must look from
the surface of the moon.

Splits and Clamps

the wind   is the soldier / they considered an enemy
                splits and clamps / soon after / the winding
                the width and horizontal of the narrow road
                going slower / change gears / high perch
the bridge   extends over / sings over / a stone to drown
                sending them to kill / maybe a lover / or child
                borders are arbitrary except when they are not
the narrow   road / empty bread baskets / shifting gears
                high noise / extends above the singing / a stone
                to sink is invisible to God / running out
                of water / forgiveness
the high   whine of the winch / dirt / it is all dry clay
                shovels are bending toward a purpose
                a longing for wet mud to hold the dead
the wind   is an army / the narrow roads / the width
                of the horizon / turn high places once
                growing into dead progress / send
                them to kill / to their deaths / frontiers
                tear and pinch
the sinking   stone is invisible / running godless
                all dirt is dry / all earth is clay / trowels
                mangled / bent toward a destination
                looking for wet mud to fill with the dead
the wind   is a ghost / is a soldier / is the dead / is
                the mud filled with bodies is the dirt
                the dirt / the dirt / the wind

Assemblage

Beaming light into utter darkness
possibilities appear to have been floated

A soft focus
capacity for self-deception

an irony lost in its precise detail
considerably less peripheral

because I'm telling the truth
The struggle against—

I didn't mean to imply—
I paranoided out—I ate it all

Are you going to discuss—?
It's relationship between the intellectual

a "comedy," "a farce [. . .]"
one pair of black gloves

eloquent testimony
a construct sufficiently supple,

even silky
professed faith

code word "incurious"
because the choices

were not choices at all

Breath Is the Measure

1

My body is flickering.
      I wake up   make sure I am breathing.
I want to write you   and say   *I don't want to die.*
      My cold hands fold underneath my pillow.
           Once, you wrote to me I saw you there and my heart
thumped.
      I saw you there I read.

                   And my heart I read.

I feel cold and colder still.   But love is not finite.   But bad habits are so
      hard to break—
           like wild horses   galloping out an open gate
and all the sudden ease with which   our fragile bodies   can possibly
      just let go

2

My body keeps flickering hot, then cold. The man I love is sleeping
next to me. I wake up to make sure he is breathing. I want to call
my friend, even though it's 3 am, and say *I want to live.* I put my cold
hands underneath my pillow. But this love is infinite.

3

My love is sleeping

                like I have killed him.

My body is cold and colder.

                For the hours

I will repeat:

                Please do not die I will say

And my heart I will say.

The Lightness of Bodies

There is a tenderness to this day, a kind of fleeting fragility
underscored by the softness of a wintry-yellow sun

spilling across a smooth wooden table and golden
light fractures across the faces of new friends

and this just after I had had the fleeting hormonal pitch black
thought that maybe now that I am older, I am just bad

at making friends. There is an achiness to my body,
a kind of keening awareness, a tenderness in my breasts

and a heaviness in my belly and it all saddens me
in the way that loneliness versus aloneness doesn't

always distinguish.
                              And I remember a different
sun-soaked day in Athens, Ohio, twenty years ago,

when I first met my friend A and it was that kind
of instantaneous friendship that you make when young.

We quickly doubled over with uncontrollable laughter,
sharing inside jokes as we pushed each other around

in a rolling cart used for transferring trays of food,
finding hilarity in everything like you do when young and beautiful

and have no worries. We were the best of friends until we liked
the same boy. I am the bad person in this story. I have never been good

enough to resist something I wanted, something pleasurable
and oh M's sweet soft lips felt so good and it was autumn in Ohio

and the leaves were   and the sun was   and we were so so so young
and our bodies were so light.

A fork drops on the floor with a pinging

sound and suddenly I'm back at this table now at an artist's residency
and we are talking about how hard it is to kill an animal for meat,

especially an animal that we have named, even if we have nick-named
the animal Sirloin with the kind of knowing, the foreshadowing

of what is to come, and the conversation turns to how removed
we are from what we eat and from there we are talking

about our own bones, and the way we become dust,
and how we can be composted or buried in a kind of disintegrating

cloth that grows into a tree and I think of my friend who almost died
even though he never mentions it and of my husband who gave me a scar

when his blood pressure scaled the heights as high as the tops
of the cathedrals shining with ice in the frozen French-Canadian city

we were in when it occurred and there is so much sunlight on this table
and we are telling stories about ashes blowing where they will—

back into someone's face, onto a sweater, or the chunk of metal
that surprises clunking out of the urn and we laugh and laugh

because what else can you do? What else can you do?

Three

How to Find Your Voice

All the members of the family come home and sit at the table. Collect their coins as tolls for the passage of time. Set them to polishing the silver. Eat with your hands full. Chew the dirt and change under the weight of soil. Collect the dough and play with Mr. Potato Head. Our bare hands shine with that awful and warm glyphosate that is supposedly perfectly safe. I use a fancy, lace-edged tea towel and elbow-length vinyl pink gloves to muffle my screams, put on my best jewelry and highest heels to take the 5th day pill with a shank. The Midwest has taught me manners. How to not look like a drug addict. How different an animal's back is from a lidded pot. Ask any 6-year-old. I fell into this endocrine anxiety disorder. Swallows, pigeons and bees are sensitive to toxins. Scientists say they have found a solution to assess the safety of animals at risk. That is, death is measured. Ask if your lover has forgotten how one should treat a heart. Measure out the pills. Measure out the poison drip by drop. Tip-top, tip-toe, as rain baffles the tin roof and sounds like loud tearing. The stained glass in the front door was sold off long ago. The ruffles on my Sunday best dress are loose and need stitching. The keening must stay inside my bee-stung cortex. I use suture cord to mend my mouth closed.

Family History

1.

What is father?
What is mother?
call out for her)
(moth cocoon)
(traitorous)
washed jeans)
pathogenic (trail)
ties) individual
autosomal recessive
(disorder) (Snoopy
with red wine stain)
pattern of inheritance
painful disorder
(my hands are
familiar to what
(define the word
use it) lines
(a pussycat
the endometrium—
again: unruly genes)
bottoms overthrow
(what is normal?)
cord, retina, kidney,
system (if you are
are you having kids)
fallopian tubes
lining the pelvis
be lifelong
priceless
keep in your small
condition can't be
alive for less)
tissue has no way
(what does not pain

(half the genes)
(dying men
Genetic encoding
of dominant traits
single-gene (acid-
disease caused by
variants (Christmas
(I) (you)
autosomal dominant
dressed as reindeer
or X/Y-linked (cuff)
(monogrammed silver)
(out of) tissue is similar
my grandmother's)
(familiar to whom?)
disorder if you are going to
the inside of the uterus—
is also called a familiar)
grows outside (disorder
(high-waisted 70s style bell
the patriarchy) a mutation
affects brain, spinal
pancreas and reproductive
a woman, everyone asks *when*
(A: *joke is on you*) ovaries,
(fig.1 like a textbook) tissue
chronic: can last for years or
(nightmare parade of
family heirlooms you should
house) (I mean womb)
cured (they burned women
thickens, breaks down, bleeds
(out) to exit the pained body
even feel like?)

becomes trapped (an animal) (no cure)
(treatments are temporary, painful)
abnormal (the canary dies)
organs stick to one another (red velvet
cake) frameshift permutation (you saw
this movie already) unexpected affect
cellular proliferation (it had Leonardo DiCaprio in it)
invasive survival potential cells multiply
uncontrollably (*Inception*) structural
chromosomal abnormalities categorized
(MC Escher) deletions, duplications
translocations, inversions, or rings
(staircases that lead nowhere)
unbalanced complements of genes
thereby causing problems
for the progeny (looping)

2.

Malleable memories
entail the most mundane
such as second-guessing
whether I really did
turn off the stove

*

Protean
Readily assuming different forms or characters;
extremely variable

(initial capital letter) of, relating to, or suggestive
of Proteus

Protanomaly, protanopia, protasis, prote-, protea,
protease, protease inhibitor, protect

See: an amoeba is a *protean* animalcule

As in: humans crawling into existence out of the muck
from single-celled organisms

*

Epigenetic memory / epigenetic inheritance
Environmental genetic changes / can be passed down
fourteen generations in *C. elegans nematodes*
(roundworms)

Epigenetic inheritance: the question is:
how long-lasting these inter-generational effects
last

*

Great, great, great grandfather: Solomon Cutler

Solomon: "Man of Peace"
Alternative spelling: *Salomon*

Related *names*: Suleiman, Sulayman, Salomão, Shlomo,
Soghomon, Salman, Zalman

Solomon is a common given name, surname derived from Aramaic

Cutler: English: occupational name for a maker of knives,
from an agent derivative of Middle English,
Old French co(u)tel, co(u)teau "knife";
Late Latin cultellus, a diminutive of culter "plowshare"

Americanized spelling of German Kottler or Kattler:
of uncertain origin

*

Existence
entity, reality, individuality, animation, duration
continuation, continuance, endurance, presence, perseverance,
permanence
essence, subsistence, survival, journey
real world, rat race, hand one is dealt, big game, the long con
something

as in: something that exists
as in: actuality
as in: being
as in: breath

*

Inheritance
uncertain origin / a set of good knives
Did I turn off the stove? Did I turn off the stove?

3.

What is daughter? (girl) (female) (me)   What is sister? (girl) (addition) (younger) (split images)   Problem with (association) (smell of gardenias) central pain increases   (value of health) Sensitivity (hot) (cold) (scent) or perception (prophetic)   Brain processes pain (being torn apart) reacts to given triggers (catch) (bracelet) (necklace) (band of painful muscles)   Test (trial) (symptoms) sets off (adorn) eleven out of nineteen (cardinal) identified body parts   Fatigue (break)   Unsatisfactory sleep (inoperative)   Cognitive problems (evidence) ongoing (chronic) (days spent watching birds at the feeder out the window) (immoveable)   May (prediction) be hereditary (memory) (body) (swimming in the lake at sunset on land my great-grandfather bought in 1934) (my grandmother's diagnosis)   Exact (solution) cause is unclear   Nucleotides (string) not divisible (disunited) by three (me) (mother) (sister)   Gene (pool) or variant expresses different signs (semiotics) (car crash) (accident) (post-traumatic) (whiplash) (variable expressivity)   Mild (merciful) manifestation or severe (excessive) complications   Mitochondrial (thread) inheritance strictly maternal (trauma) only egg cells (incite) developing embryos   Females pass on (track) mutations to offspring (epigenetic)   Fathers (men) do not give the disorders (confusion) to their daughters (xy) to their sons (y)   May take (cheat) years of painful (inflict) tests   What is autoimmune? (against)   What is immunity? (inviolability) (the portrait of my great-grandmother in my childhood bedroom) (she holds a gardenia)   The exact mouth I see in the mirror

Sea, Salt, Mineral, Bones

If a woman is a mother then that is all that she is allowed to be
if a woman is not a mother then she is a vessel to be filled

until she is no longer a woman but a childless womb
A woman is only as soft as she once was as hard

as she can be but she is not allowed to be too soft
or too hard   just ripe enough for a man to be pleased

A woman is a shell a soft pearl pink thing
a hard outer skin but a woman is not a weight

to hold on to unless a man says so
then she can be the sinking, the ball

of the foot pressing into soft soil
like the snail shells circling and circling

that crunch in the loamy garden soil that we reach
into that we dig into the dirt with our fingers

And the worms come to the surface when it rains
Water is something we all need

And a woman has grown all of us   Which is maybe
why men cannot be still enough or soft enough

or gentle enough because they
cannot do what every mother has done

split her body in two   And a man is not
circled shells   But a man can be soft   gentle

can lie down next to a woman and weep
feel circled in tenderness   But a man does not

stay in that circle   A man wants to go down
To stay down   To learn gentleness a different way

to be   to become   But he he he he he   will try
and he will breathe in and out and match his breath

to the woman sleeping next to him   He will try
A man will try to become like a woman

Or maybe a woman will try to become like a man
But too often this will end in a violence

which is a man who cannot have what he thinks
he deserves   a woman's body   is

the rocks the sand the salt the sky the clouds the sea
and the circle that is the sun that we cannot look at directly

is a woman who is giving birth or not at all like that but
a moon of gravity that pulls us all to live to breathe

to bathe in the waves   the salt inside of us
And a man will come close to try and tear back

inside of a woman   And all that softening
like wet sand between toes   You feel that right now

when you read these words   that softness   drenched
earth underneath your feet   and it is all left over mineral,

sea, salt, animal, bones   The salt the salt the salt
skin a beginning of when of when of when of when

a mother becomes a mother a woman becomes a lover
and a man is neither   and   the soft pouch of skin

we began in   we lay our head on a belly   We want
to return through the belly   a softness   but we cannot

un-knot   the knot is the cord is the stretch is the lover
is the literal part of the longing   the knot

the untying the retying   the cord that will try
to untie that will want and not want   to be knotted

that is the woman   who is always the tangled knot
from belly to soft belly, and the first cry when it is cut

Collector

He is clearing out his ex-wife's bookshelf for her. Moving his books one by one, stacking them spine-side up in sturdy cardboard boxes, tenderly, the same way his hands learn my backbones, wrist bones, ankle bones. He is careful with what he loves. He calls to me, *Have you read* _____? I answer yes or no, pull the quilt up near my ears, move closer to the warmth of the dog. It is just starting to turn cold. He is reminded of something past with each new cover. She will come and take the empty shell, fill up the space with her new life. Stand in front of this red house again, walk in and gather her leftover pieces from the corners. I imagine her looking at my things, smelling my pink perfume, picking up my hairbrush, seeing my long red hair. I am the spirit of this house now. Later, I'll hear him downstairs, sliding the boxes from one side of the room to the other. I know this is a task that cannot be hurried. Upstairs, I'll be folding clean clothes and tucking them into drawers. From basket to dresser, with each footfall I make, the old wooden floorboards sing.

Hold

This night, in separate cities for different reasons than usual, I want to bridge this space between you and me in the same way our mouths collapse our bodies together, the same way our arms fold over the small spaces where our bodies gap in embracing, and press you against me. You are doing something I don't like to think of you doing alone: watching your mother die. Later, you will tell me how you were looking out of the hospital window at the city below, imagining what each person might understand under the lamp of their own light, and in that instant you spoke out loud to me, forgetting that I wasn't there, and I will tell you how in that moment I was lying in my bed, holding my breath to better hear your voice.

Refraction

My husband, born in 1949, could never have imagined a future
where so much precious time is spent creating passwords

with a symbol, a capital letter, without repeating combinations
we can remember. *Cut the fat* we say, meaning to trim away excess

but everything seems to take longer now at the same time that saying
I love you travels via satellite across the world in half a second

give or take the weather conditions in space. *Don't take any wooden
nickels* and *Write when you get work* were things my grandfather

said as we were leaving after Sunday dinner. The antique table
where we break our bread now is polished by the hands

of so many who came before us. *Bless this food* we say, meaning
Bless us and when we stop to exchange pleasantries on the street

we talk about the weather: *It's hot. It's humid. It looks like snow.*
We mention feeling the rain coming in the ache of our joints.

We point to the stars and say *Look. There. The moon, the moon*,
my three-year-old niece exclaims. She continues to wonder

at this bright globe in the sky. Curtains hang to keep out
the sun, the moonlight, the eyes of strangers. Silence

in the dark is something tangible that we either want
or fear. We have filled up dark space with light pollution

and we must now go to the wilderness to feel wildness.
A moment considered *Stolen in time* is one that we enjoyed.

Some people close their eyes and see numbers, others words,
some see pictures, others only colors. And yet we can still

communicate across distance with words like *Welcome, friend,*
love. We long for the people we have lost and we miss people

we don't see. Have you ever come upon your lover and looked
at them objectively before you realized they were your lover?

Can you remember how your lover looked to you before
they became beloved? Can we catch ourselves unawares?

The closest we can imagine is reflection in still water, refraction,
the water a veil, our self-consciousness always the anvil.

Fulcrum

My body is reappearing. My lover has reappeared. My pain has disappeared. My lover is my pain and not my lover. Balance is where you place your order. My lover is not a leaver, but a lever. My lover is an embrace, a bolster, a cantilever, a grip, a strut, a vice. My lover is a jack. A boost, a bring up, a construct, a construction, an elevation, an establishment, an exaltation, a heave, a hike, a hoist, a holdup, a jump over, a mount up, a place. My lover is gone. My pain has reappeared. My pain is my body and also not my lover. Balance is the place to place your order. My lover is an embrace, a console, a consolation, a handle, a rib. My pain is gone, my body is back, my lover is my pain and not my lover. Balance is where you place your order. Begging my lover is not escape. My lover is an anchor, extension, grip, suspension, vice. My lover is gone. The pain has recurred. My pain is my body, not my lover. My body is a vice. My lover's ability is a fix. My lover is my worst chronic best. My body is mine to mine and mind. My pain is my own body. My lover is a body, is not pain, is not my body, is my body wanting.

All My Friends Post Their Loved Ones' Death Notices Online

Those private, secret moments
        becoming something   we need
to share with anyone   everyone   all our words
out in the world   now a way to staunch the wound—
        to heal
               unexpected
loss.

*

So many days   I see
someone your age, or younger, and I think
           it could have been   you
just
gone.

Your words disappearing.
Pages of you left behind. Lines and lines
               letters and all the text
that could wrap or be   wound
      around the two of us   thousands of times

over.

*

Here, away from you
I send selfies like postcards
trying to cast a net
               a string on the kite of me
that will catch in your fingers.

             Often, I think about your
hands.

The way   they move through the air when you talk
the way they move   over me
and I regret all the years we weren't in touch
all the time   wasted

                                        not touching.

I think about your body.
I know you think about mine.
What fragile   fragile   fragile
tender thoughts.
          And I don't want to lose you.

                              *

The stars across the sky
always   the leaving   at sunrise.
                    The waves
making lines
          I count on the shore.

*

Salt sticks to skin
                    desire like   so much sand
time like   so much water
                    and we are always
always on this beach
                    dying of thirst.

                              *

Do we have much
          do we have   how much   do we have
how much   how much   how much   how much
time?
there is never enough
          there is no end
                    to this   wanting

64

I want
           to ask
I want
           you
I want
                           more
                                I want
how much
           I want

These Tender Days

1.

Laura is gone now
and I was trying to finish this poem about her daughter
as a surprise for her
But I forgot
put it away in a drawer to get out later
thinking I had all the time in the world
And now   and now
and now

2.

Anna
        on her paddleboard
the middle of the lake
        She balances, poised on still water, two long legs, posed
Heron-like
holds steady, her platinum blonde hair is white seagull wing in the sunlig
Her laughter laps at the shore

3.

Anna's laugh is her mother's
        in the same way water streams
melodies we play in the mind
        until until until
we see each other again
        the water is   the water is   the water is
the way voices carry over
        from one side to the other
winter's frost to freeze
        to crack to thaw
the spring's current
        flowing
endless

4.

We've lost so much
and we wonder

at the ways in which
we manage

to just   go on
breathing

days of sun
clouds

birds calling
The lake

a mirror
reflects sky

our own two hands
press together

steepled in awe
its own kind of prayer

we press a pebble
against our palm

against our lips
a feather floats past

trembling
the surface

the circling of water
where the stone drops

from our fingers
reminds us of all

the ways we could be
can be   will be

gentle
with each other

A reminder of how
to reach across the divide

and say
I love you, my friend

I am here for you
And maybe that tenderness

will be enough to get us through
this, one second and then

another

Blackbird

Time ticks in seconds into years without notice. We are so busy leaping into rosier future after rosy future after pink future, we don't even remember to forget. Let this page of ink-black words be a marker for us, be witness to how we grasp each other's warmth with both hands, stop to watch the red leaves fall off the maple tree, look up at the night sky, notice the yellowing moon is waxing, is full, is waning. Let time remind us how fragile are the bodies we hold.

I lean my elbows on the windowsill and look down at the garden. You are working a patch of black dirt with your hands, the dog stops and sniffs the air, the soft wings of a new blackbird rustle in a tender breeze. You look up at me and smile before you place the tomato plant in the ground, pinching the earth around its stalk. The smell of peonies drifts in the open window as I unwind my hair, letting it unfurl toward you like new roots.

Notes

"A Girl is Always a Body" is indebted to the poem "When You Are a Ghost, I'll Also Love Your Shadow" by Kelli Russell Agodon.

"Good Girl" is indebted to the book *City of Rust* by Rochelle Hurt.

"X-ray" borrows its title from the poem "X-ray" by Kathleen Mc-Gookey.

"Hands Falling Like Two Birds" is indebted to the poem "Confession 6" by Nin Andrews.

"The Graces Prefer Those Who Wear Flowers" borrows its title from a phrase by Sappho.

"We Measure by the Second Hand Circling" borrows the phrase "tender buttons" from Gertrude Stein's book title *Tender Buttons*.

"Violent Wonder" is written after the poem "Meditation at Lagunitas" by Robert Hass.

"Murmuration" is indebted to the artwork "Elevate" by Stephen Yusko.

"Assemblage" is indebted to the artwork "Curious Theater" by Linda Mayer and to the novel *Miami* by Joan Didion.

"All My Friends Post Their Loved Ones' Death Notices Online" is a variation on the title "All my Friends' Barbecues Need Attending" by Carrie Oeding.

Acknowledgments

I wish to thank my family, especially Meredith Deierling, Addie Deierling, Sharyn Fuller, Mark Fuller, Adam Deierling, Alison Rich, Mike Rich, Ashlie Miltner, and Ross Miltner. My gratitude to the following people for inspiration, reading, support, love, friendship, wine, and/or lots of coffee: Angie Mazakis, Michelle Lewis, Karen Schubert, Andrew Rihn, Rick Campbell, Jasper, Nicole Robinson, Bob Kunzinger, Bill Black, Kristen Lillvis, Anna Barie, Brian Young, Shannon Young, Matt Mackey, Claire Fabre, Sophie Bocquet, Rebekah Taylor-Wiseman, Kristin Love, Melanie Murphy, John Howard, Aubrey Crosby, Barbara Sabol, Jane Varley, Donna Long, Nin Andrews, Christopher Citro, Angela Sorby, Caki Wilkinson, and the VSC Feb 2020 crew—especially Kate Laster who so generously shared her artwork for our broadside. My appreciation for the time and space to Wellspring House, Wassaic Project, and Vermont Studio Center. A special thanks to Dr. Ross K. Tangedal, Director & Publisher of Cornerstone Press, and the team of students (especially Brett Hill, Julia Kaufman, and Carolyn Czerwinski), who helped me bring this book into the world.

* * *

The author wishes to thank the editors or organizers of the following journals, magazines, chapbooks, anthologies, and exhibitions in which the following pieces were published:

JOURNALS AND MAGAZINES

Amethyst Review: "We Measure by the Second-Hand Circling"

Birdcoat: "Calibrations" and "How to Abandon a City"

Buried Letter Press: "The Cherry Tree Blessing"

Calliope: "Shelf Life"

Cloudbank: "A Girl is Always a Body"

Gris-Gris: A Journal of Literature, Culture, and the Arts: "Good Girl"

Into the Void: "Almost Perfect Stillness"

Panoply: A Literary Zine: "Endurance"

Pedestal Magazine: "Breath is the Measure"

Pretty Owl Poetry: "Violent Wonder"

Sheila-Na-Gig: "Sara Says Ghosts Are Real"

Slush Pile Magazine: "This Resembles a Funeral Ritual"

Streetcake (UK): "All My Friends Post Their Loved Ones' Death Notices Online"

The Hopper: "Fractals of Skin Hunger"

The Fourth River: "The River Will Bear You"

Yes Poetry: "Metamorphosis"

Zoetic Press: "Collapse"

ANTHOLOGY

But You Don't Look Sick: The Real Life Adventures of Fibro Bitches, Lupus Warriors, and other Super Heroes Battling Invisible Illness (Indie Blu(e) Publishing): "Family History"

CHAPBOOK

Tender the Body (Spare Change Press): "Blackbird," "Collector," and "Hold"

ART EXHIBITIONS

Vermont Studio Center Art Gallery, 2020: "A Girl is Always a Body" poetry and print broadside by Kate Laster

Rust: Recycled Metal Sculpture Art and Poetry Exhibition, Cleveland Heights Arts Gallery, 2022: Poem display of "Assemblage" and "Murmuration"

The author would like to thank the following journals and contests which recognized pieces included in this book:

Awards and Recognitions

Winner, Summer Poetry Contest, *Gris-Gris Magazine*, 2020, for "Good Girl"

Editor's Choice Award, *Panoply: A Literary Zine*, 2020, for "Endurance"

Finalist, Great Midwest Poetry Contest, *Midwest Review*, 2020, for "Good Girl"

Honorable mention, International Women Who Write Poetry Contest, 2013, for "Shelf Life."

Selectee (juried), Vermont Studio Center Gallery Broadside Exhibition, June 2020, for "A Girl is Always a Body"

MOLLY FULLER is the author of *For Girls Forged by Lightning: Prose & Other Poems* (2017), and two poetry chapbooks, *Tender the Body* (2013) and *The Neighborhood Psycho Dreams of Love* (2013). She has been awarded Editor's Choice by *Panoplyzine* (February 2020), Finalist for the Great Midwest Poetry Contest by *Midwest Review* (March 2020), and winner of *Gris-Gris Literary Journal's* Summer 2020 Poetry Contest (September 2020).

She has previously been short-listed for Nunum's Flash Fiction Contest (Winter 2019), nominated for a Pushcart Prize by Pithead Chapel (November 2019), awarded an Artist's Grant by Vermont Studio Center (February 2019), awarded an Artist's Grant by Wassaic Project (March & April 2019), awarded Semi-Finalist status in the Adrift Short Story Contest Driftwood Press (2019), a Semi-Finalist for *The Florida Review* Jeanne Leiby Memorial Chapbook Award (2016), First place in the LIT Youngstown Storygami Contest (2016), and a Finalist for the Key West Literary Seminar Emerging Writer Award (2015).

www.ingramcontent.com/pod-product-compliance
Lightning Source LLC
Chambersburg PA
CBHW030505130626
46549CB00007B/2863

979898696638 0